Excellence

A Choral Dialectic
for Unaccompanied SATB Choir
and an Animal Choir

- Secretary Michael

I0164938

"Excellence" Choral Dialectic
by Secretary Michael

ISBN: 978-1-888712-40-7
- Original -

All works by Secretary Michael have been placed into the Public Domain. They may be freely copied and performed.

What is a Choral Dialectic?

A "choral dialectic" is a four-movement choral work (with or without instruments) in which a rational argument about any subject is battled-out musically. There's only one rule: every choral dialectic must use the following four titles for its four movements:

1. "**PRINCIPLE**"
Each dialectic begins with a statement of some sort. This will be the subject matter for the entire work. Oftentimes the statement is an ideal - an expression of how something might be in a perfect world.

2. "**ARGUMENT**"
In this movement, the "Principle" begins its journey through the meat grinder. The Argument's job is to pick apart the principle, either supporting it or challenging it.

3. "**COUNTERARGUMENT**"
In this movement, the "Principle" gets supported or challenged again, but this time from a contrasting perspective. If the previous argument was sweet, this one will probably be sour. If the previous was about abundance, this one will probably be about scarcity.

4. "**RESOLUTION**"
Now that the "Principle" has been analyzed from different angles, some sort of final understanding will have to emerge. Maybe there will be growth, a new way of being, a new way of living in the world, a new "Principle". Or maybe not.

Machinists Union Press
web: www.machinistsunion.org
email: twimfina@gmail.com

Excellence

Duration: Less than 13 minutes

Principle

(from the "Excellence" choral dialectic)

Secretary Michael
(melody from a traditional Irish tune)

♩=96

F Dm7 B♭ C7 F
S
We are a choir___ for e - v'ry - one.
A
We are a choir for e - v'ry - one.
T
We are a choir for e - v'ry - one.
B
We are a choir for e - v'ry - one.
4
Gm Am B♭ C(sus4) C
S
Work - ing to - ge - ther to get the song sung.
A
Work - ing to - ge - ther to get the song sung.
T
Work - ing to - ge - ther to get the song sung.
B
Work - ing to - ge - ther to get the song sung.

PD All works by Secretary Michael have been placed into the Public Domain. They may be freely copied and performed.

8
F Am Dm B♭
S
We all be - lieve,___ so - pra - no to bass,
A
We all be - lieve, so - pra - no to bass,
T
We all be - lieve,___ so - pra - no to bass,
B
We all be - lieve, so - pra - no to bass,

12
F Dm B♭/C F
S
that e - v'ry sing - er should be gi - ven a place.
A
that e - v'ry sing - er should be gi - ven a place.
T
that e - v'ry sing - er should be gi - ven a place.
B
that e - v'ry sing - er shoud be gi - ven a place.

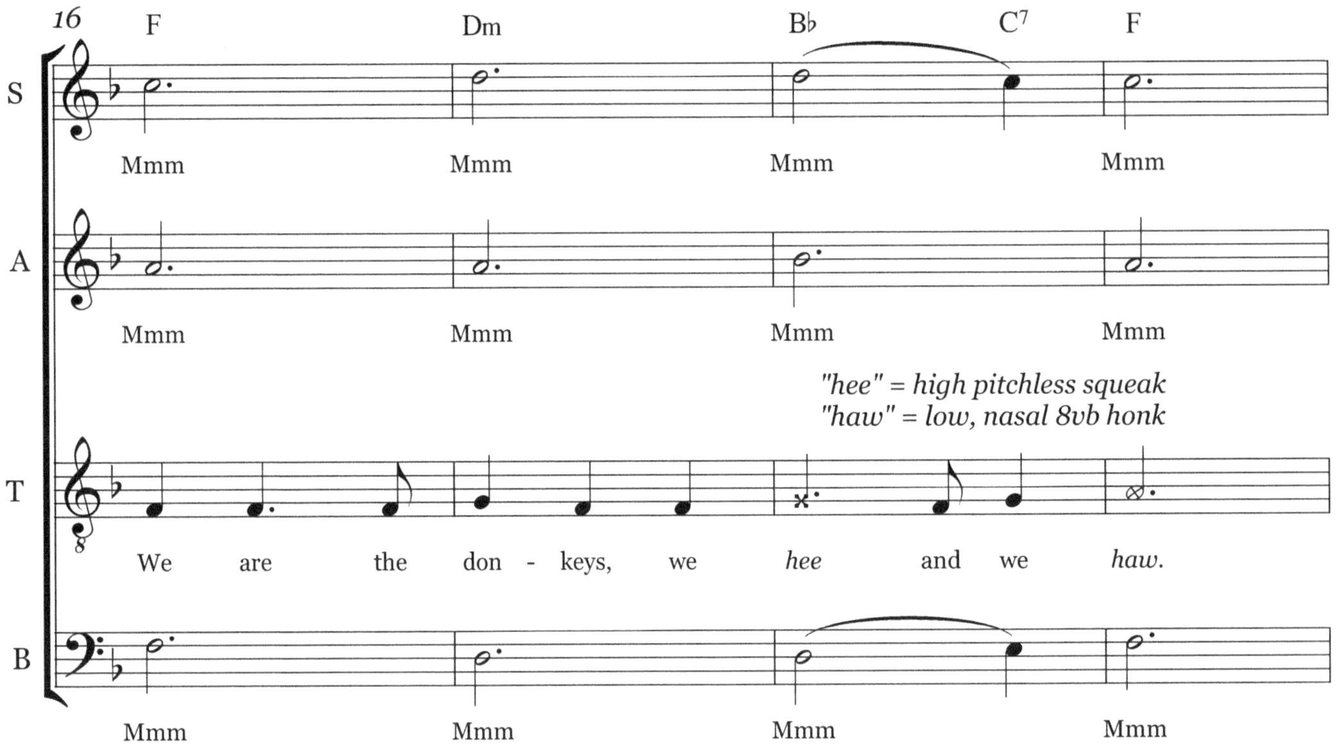
16
F Dm B♭ C7 F
S
Mmm Mmm Mmm Mmm
A
Mmm Mmm Mmm Mmm
"hee" = high pitchless squeak
"haw" = low, nasal 8vb honk
T
We are the don - keys, we *hee* and we *haw*.
B
Mmm Mmm Mmm Mmm

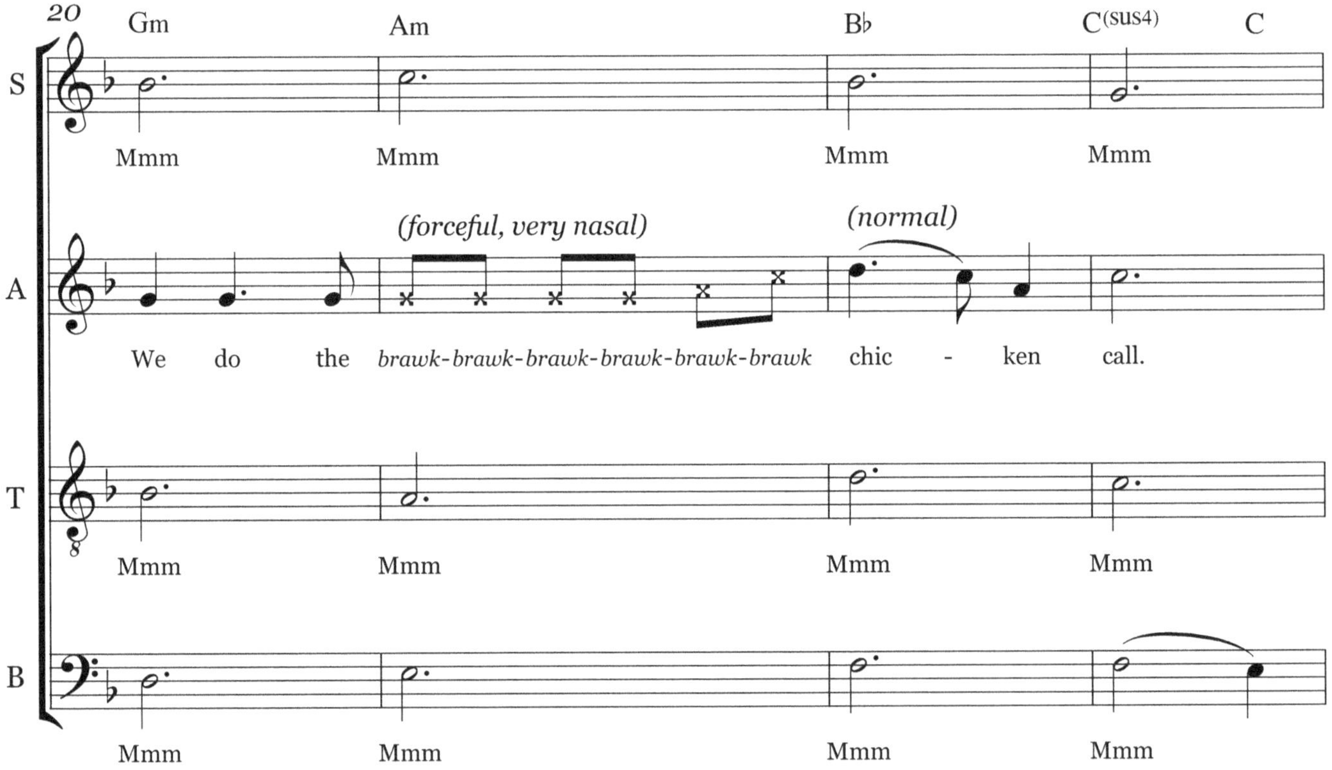
20
Gm Am B♭ C(sus4) C
S
Mmm Mmm Mmm Mmm
(forceful, very nasal)
(normal)
A
We do the *brawk-brawk-brawk-brawk-brawk-brawk* chic - ken call.
T
Mmm Mmm Mmm Mmm
B
Mmm Mmm Mmm Mmm

"hoo" = thrown falsetto
24
F
Am
Dm
B♭
(normal)
S
We are the owls, we hoo - hoo - hoo - hoo.
A
Mmm Mmm Mmm Mmm
T
Mmm Mmm Mmm Mmm
B
Mmm Mmm Mmm Mmm
28
F
Dm
B♭/C
F
S
Mmm Mmm Mmm Mmm
A
Mmm Mmm Mmm Mmm
T
Mmm Mmm Mmm Mmm
B
We are the cows, we moo moo - moo.
(scoop into each of the 3 moo's)

32
F Dm7 B♭ C7 F
S
All of us dif - f'rent as dif - f'rent can be.
A
All of us dif - f'rent as dif - f'rent can be.
T
All of us dif - f'rent as dif - f'rent can be.
B
All of us dif - f'rent as dif - f'rent can be.
36
Gm Am B♭ C(sus4) C
S
All of us search - ing for har - mo - ny.
A
All of us search - ing for har - mo - ny.
T
All of us search - ing for har - mo - ny.
B
All of us seach - ing for har - mo - ny.

40
F
Am
Dm
B♭
S
Bring on the cac - kles, the bel - lows and shouts,
A
Bring on the cac - kles, the bel - lows and shouts,
T
Bring on the cac - kles, the bel - lows and shouts,
B
Bring on the cac - kles, the bel - lows and shouts,
44
F
Dm
B♭/C
F
S
We'll find a way to make it work out.
A
We'll find a way to make it work out.
T
We'll find a way to make it work out.
B
We'll find a way to make it work out.

48
F Dm B♭ C7 F Gm Am
S
Mmm Mmm Mmm Mmm Mmm Mmm
(tremolo)
A
Mmm Mmm Mmm Mmm We are the baa
(forceful, nasal)
T
We are the ducks, quack-quack we keep beat. Mmm Mmm
B
Mmm Mmm Mmm Mmm Mmm Mmm
54
B♭ C(sus4) C F Am Dm
S
Mmm Mmm We are the birds, we (whistle)
(normal)
A
sheep. Mmm Mmm Mmm
T
Mmm Mmm Mmm Mmm Mmm
B
Mmm Mmm Mmm Mmm Mmm

59
B♭
F
Dm
B♭/C
F
S
chirp.
Mmm
Mmm
Mmm
Mmm
A
Mmm
Mmm
Mmm
Mmm
Mmm
T
Mmm
Mmm
Mmm
Mmm
Mmm
B
Mmm
We are the pigs, we
(inhaled snorts)
burp.
(staccato whistle, optionally embellished with ottava and avian coloratura)
64
F
Dm7
Birds
(whistled...)
(whistled...)
Sheep (Mel.)
(bleating tremolo)
Baa - Baa - - Baa - Baa - - Baa -
(nasal quacking)
Ducks
Quack - quack - quack - quack - quack
Quack - quack - quack - quack - quack
(inhaled snorts)
Pigs

66
B♭
C7
F
Birds
(whistled...)
(whistled...)
Sheep (Mel.)
Baa - - Baa - Baa.
Ducks
Quack - quack - quack - quack Quack - quack Quack - quack - quack - quack Quack Hee -
Pigs
* * * * * * * * * * *
(falsetto "Hoo-Hoo-Hoo"; each "Hoo" ends with a drop in pitch)
68
Gm
Am
Owls
Hoo Hoo Hoo Hoo Hoo Hoo
(nasal cackling, scooping into last "BRAWK")
Chkns
Brawk - brawk - brawk - brawk BRAWK! Brawk - brawk - brawk - brawk BRAWK!
(squeaky high "Hee" followed by low nasal honk)
Dkeys
Haw Hee - Haw Hee -
(scoop into pitch from below)
Cows (Mel.)
Moo - Moo - Moo - Moo - - Moo -

70
B♭
C(sus4)
C
Owls
Hoo Hoo Hoo Hoo Hoo Hoo
Chkns
Brawk - brawk - brawk - brawk BRAWK! Brawk - brawk - brawk - brawk - brawk - brawk
Dkeys
Haw Hee - Haw
Cows (Mel.)
Moo - - Moo - Moo.
72
F
Am
Dm
B♭
S
Work - ing to - ge - ther to get the song sung.
A
Work - ing to - ge - ther to get the song sung.
T
Work - ing to - ge - ther to get the song sung.
B
Work - ing to - ge - ther to get the song sung.

76
F
Dm
B♭/C
F
S
A
T
B
We are a choir for e - v'ry - one.
We are a choir for e - v'ry - one.
We are a choir for e - v'ry - one.
We are a choir for e - v'ry - one.
MONOTONE MOOSE (a tenor) enters the stage, which alarms everybody;
His voice is harsh and impudent; the SHEEP are able to translate for him
80
Monotone Moose
MM
Blah Blah Blah-Blah Blah Blah Blah Blah-Blah Blah
(interrupting)
Sheep Translators
Sheep Choir
He says "Ex - cuse me Choir for
85
MM
Blah Blah Blah - Blah Blah
Sheep Choir
E-v'ry-one, I don't mean to dis - rupt.
I'm a
90
(choir gasps)
Sheep Choir
moose and I'm a mo - no - tone and I'd like to sign up.

Argument

(from the "Excellence" choral dialectic)

Secretary Michael

PD All works by Secretary Michael have been placed into the Public Domain. They may be freely copied and performed.

9
Am
C7
F
Dm
S
one of the e - lite. No "hee" or "haw" can have a flaw, each
A
one of the e - lite. "hee" or "haw" can have a flaw, each
T
one of the e - lite. "hee" or "haw" can have a flaw, each
B
one of the e - lite. "hee" or "haw" can have a flaw, each

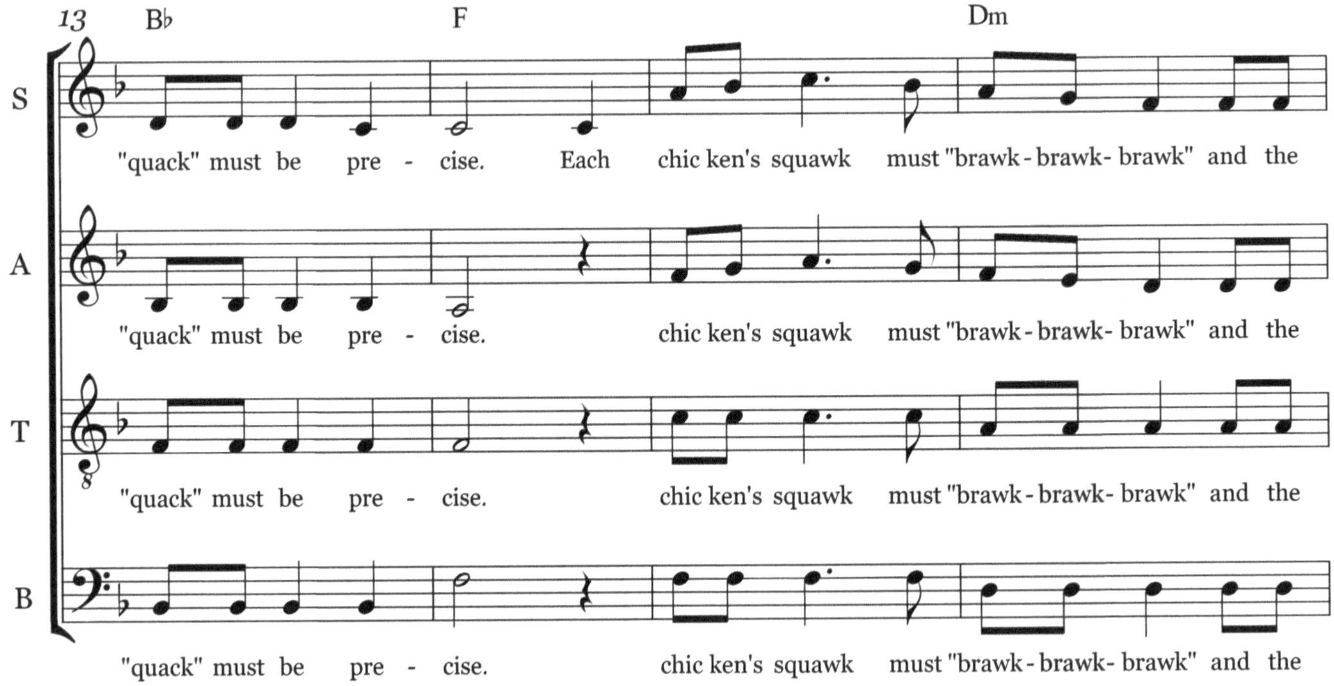
13
B♭
F
Dm
S
"quack" must be pre - cise. Each chic ken's squawk must "brawk - brawk - brawk" and the
A
"quack" must be pre - cise. chic ken's squawk must "brawk - brawk - brawk" and the
T
"quack" must be pre - cise. chic ken's squawk must "brawk - brawk - brawk" and the
B
"quack" must be pre - cise. chic ken's squawk must "brawk - brawk - brawk" and the

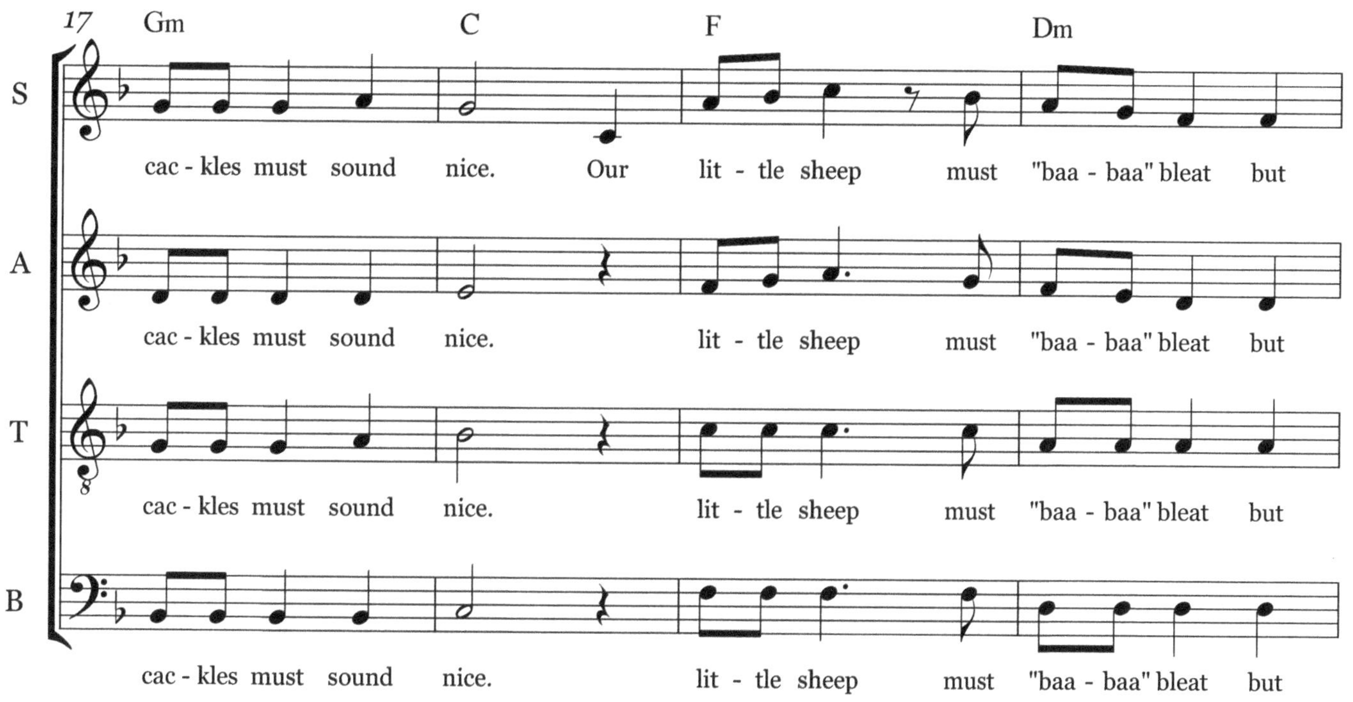
17
Gm C F Dm
S
cac - kles must sound nice. Our lit - tle sheep must "baa - baa" bleat but
A
cac - kles must sound nice. lit - tle sheep must "baa - baa" bleat but
T
cac - kles must sound nice. lit - tle sheep must "baa - baa" bleat but
B
cac - kles must sound nice. lit - tle sheep must "baa - baa" bleat but

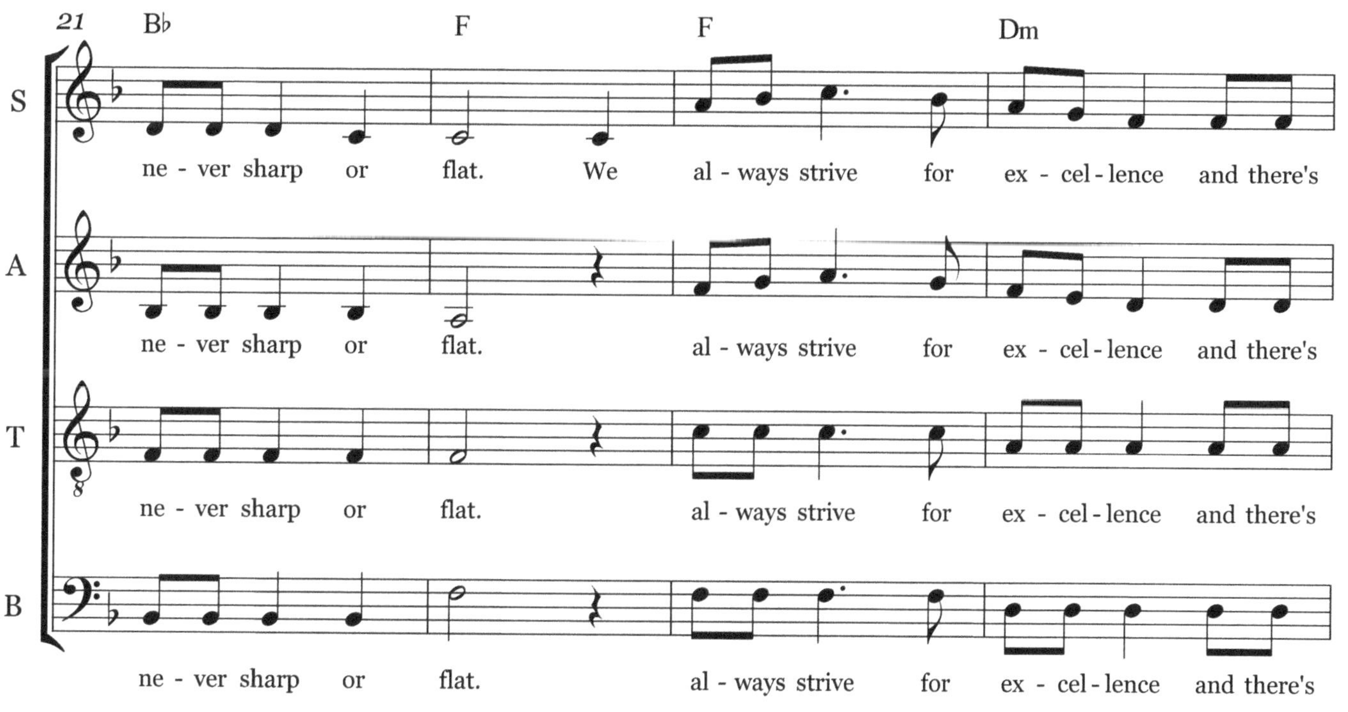
21
B♭ F F Dm
S
ne - ver sharp or flat. We al - ways strive for ex - cel - lence and there's
A
ne - ver sharp or flat. al - ways strive for ex - cel - lence and there's
T
ne - ver sharp or flat. al - ways strive for ex - cel - lence and there's
B
ne - ver sharp or flat. al - ways strive for ex - cel - lence and there's

25
Gm C F C C+
S A T B
no-thing wrong with that. We're a choir of ex - cel - lence. There are

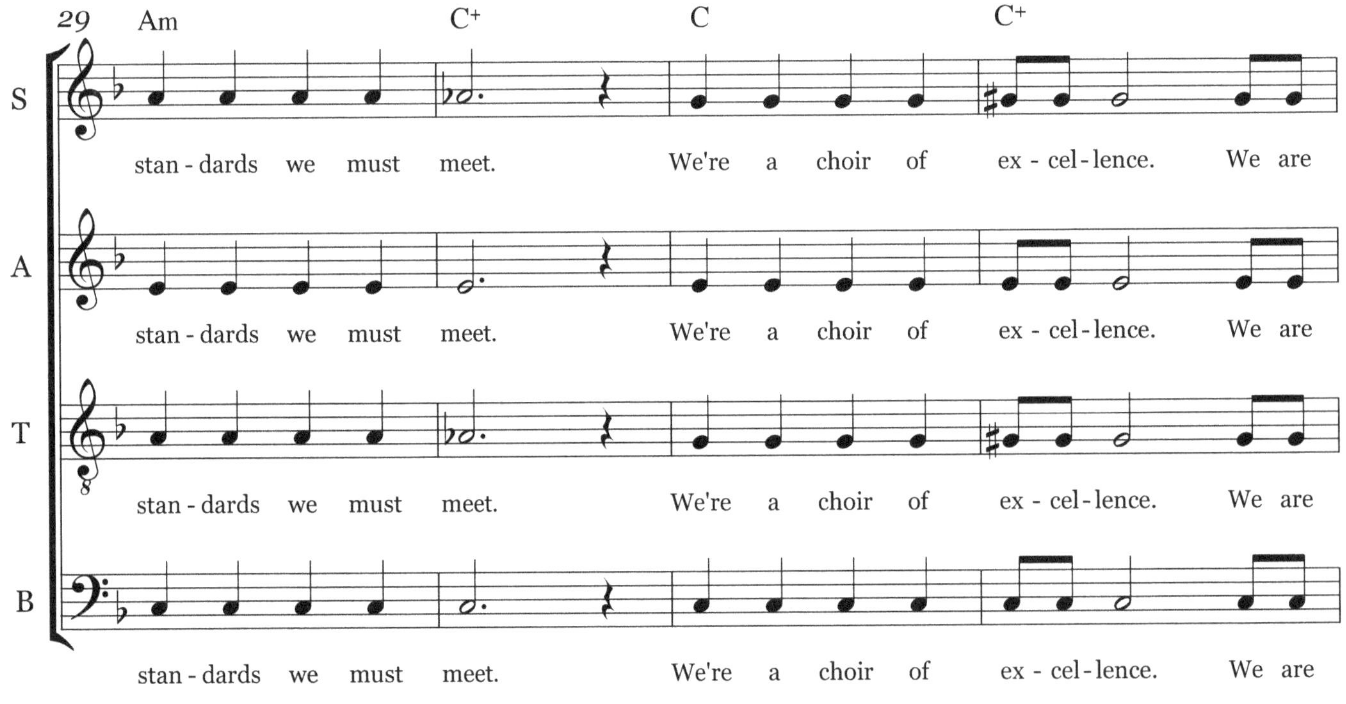
29
Am C+ C C+
S A T B
stan - dards we must meet. We're a choir of ex - cel - lence. We are

33
Am C7 F Dm
S A T B
one of the e - lite. Each "moo - oo - oo", each "hoo - oo - oo" we

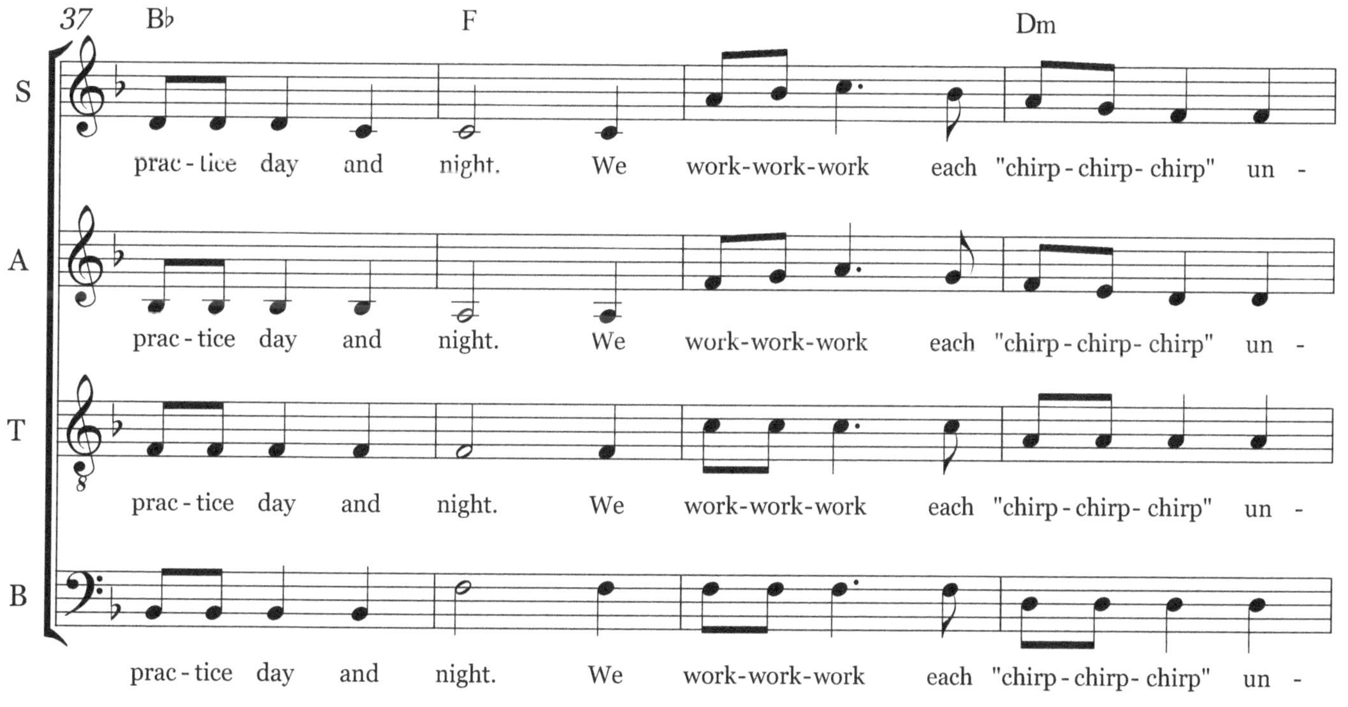
37
B♭ F Dm
S A T B
prac - tice day and night. We work-work-work each "chirp - chirp - chirp" un -

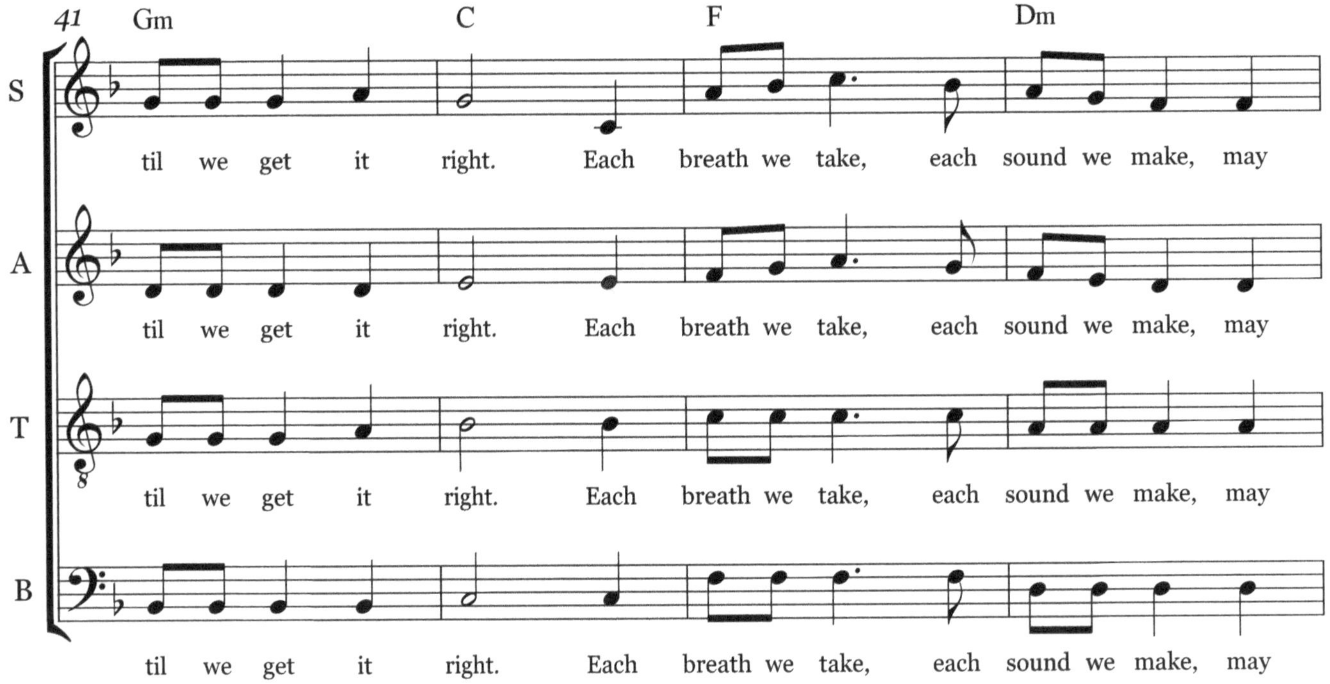
41
Gm C F Dm
S
til we get it right. Each breath we take, each sound we make, may
A
til we get it right. Each breath we take, each sound we make, may
T
til we get it right. Each breath we take, each sound we make, may
B
til we get it right. Each breath we take, each sound we make, may

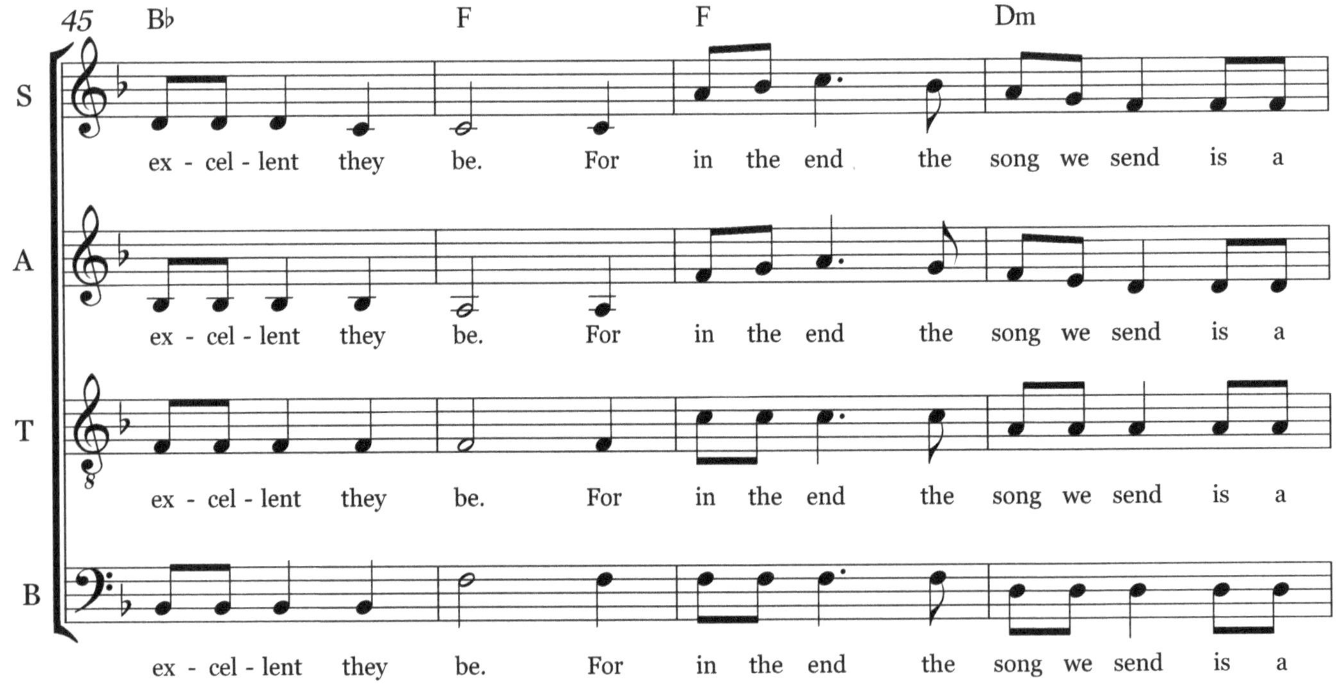
45
B♭ F F Dm
S
ex - cel - lent they be. For in the end the song we send is a
A
ex - cel - lent they be. For in the end the song we send is a
T
ex - cel - lent they be. For in the end the song we send is a
B
ex - cel - lent they be. For in the end the song we send is a

49
Gm C F C C+
S
piece of you and me. We're a choir of ex - cel - lence. There are
A
piece of you and me. We're a choir of ex - cel - lence. There are
T
piece of you and me. We're a choir of ex - cel - lence. There are
B
piece of you and me. We're a choir of ex - cel - lence. There are
53
Am C+ C C+
S
stan - dards we must meet. We're a choir of ex - cel - lence. We are
A
stan - dards we must meet. We're a choir of ex - cel - lence. We are
T
stan - dards we must meet. We're a choir of ex - cel - lence. We are
B
stan - dards we must meet. We're a choir of ex - cel - lence. We are

Animal Choir *

(Sheep and Ducks have the melody)

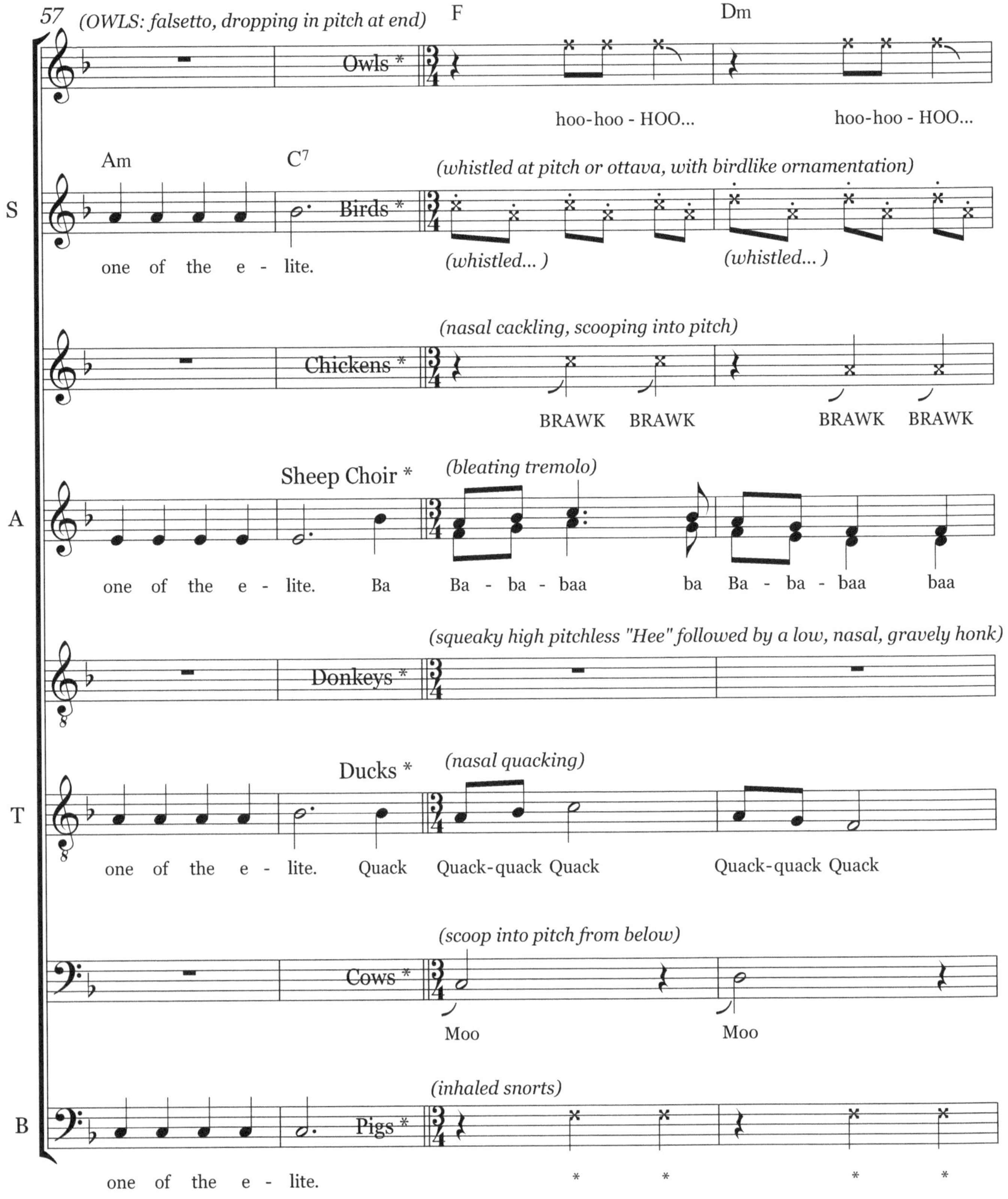

** Most animals cannot be categorized as S, A, T, or B. Singers should choose their own animal.*

61
B♭
F
Owls
hoo-hoo - HOO...
hoo-hoo - HOO...
Birds
(whistled...)
(whistled...)
(whistled...)
Chkns
BRAWK BRAWK
BRAWK BRAWK
BRAWK BRAWK
Sheep Choir
Ba - ba - baa baa Baa Baa Ba - ba - baa ba
Dkeys
Hee-Haw
Ducks
Quack-quack Quack Quack Quack Quack-quack Quack
Cows
Moo
Moo
Moo
Pigs
* * * *

64
Dm
Gm
C
Owls
hoo-hoo - HOO...
hoo-hoo - HOO...
Birds
(whistled...)
(whistled...)
(whistled...)
Chkns
BRAWK BRAWK
BRAWK BRAWK
BRAWK BRAWK
Sheep Choir
Ba - ba - baa baa
Ba - ba - baa baa
Baa baa
Dkeys
Hee-Haw
Ducks
Quack-quack Quack
Quack-quack Quack Quack
Quack
Cows
Moo
Moo
Moo
Pigs
* *
* *

67
F
Dm
B♭
Owls
hoo - hoo - HOO...
hoo - hoo - HOO...
Birds
(whistled...)
(whistled...)
(whistled...)
Chkns
BRAWK BRAWK
BRAWK BRAWK
BRAWK BRAWK
Sheep Choir
Ba - ba - baa ba
Ba - ba - baa baa
Ba - ba - baa baa
Dkeys
Ducks
Quack-quack Quack
Quack-quack Quack
Quack-quack Quack Quack
Cows
Moo
Moo
Moo
Pigs
* *
* *

70
F
Owls
hoo - hoo - HOO...
hoo - hoo - HOO...
Birds
(whistled...)
(whistled...)
Chkns
BRAWK BRAWK
BRAWK BRAWK
Sheep Choir
F
Baa
Baa
Ba - ba - baa ba
Dkeys
Hee - Haw
Ducks
Quack
Quack - quack Quack
Cows
Moo
Moo
Pigs
* * * *

72
Dm
Gm
C7
F
Owls
hoo - hoo - HOO...
HOO...
Birds
(whistled...)
(whistled...)
Chkns
BRAWK BRAWK
BRAWK BRAWK BRAWK
Sheep Choir
Ba - ba - baa baa
Ba - ba - baa baa
Baa
Dkeys
Ducks
Quack-quack Quack
Quack-quack Quack Quack
Quack
Cows
Moo
Moo
Moo
F
Pigs
* *
*

Counterargument

(from the "Excellence" choral dialectic)

Secretary Michael

Reflective, Not Rushed

1
F F F+ Dm
S
But there's a dif-f'rent kind of ex-cel-lence where the sing - ers make the
A
dif-f'rent kind of ex-cel-lence where the sing - ers make the
T
dif-f'rent kind of ex-cel-lence where the sing - ers make the
B
dif-f'rent kind of ex-cel-lence where the sing - ers make the
6
F+ F F+ Dm G
S
choice Not to sing the lies and win the prize, but to hear each o-ther's voice. There's a
A
choice sing the lies and win the prize, but to hear each o-ther's voice.
T
choice sing the lies and win the prize, but to hear each o-ther's voice.
B
choice sing the lies and win the prize, but to hear each o-ther's voice.

All works by Secretary Michael have been placed into the Public Domain. They may be freely copied and performed.

11
F F+ Dm F+ F
S
dif-f'rent kind of ex-cel lence that's as strong as it can be. But it doe-sn't sound like
A
dif-f'rent kind of ex-cel lence that's as strong as it can be. doe-sn't sound like
T
dif-f'rent kind of ex-cel lence that's as strong as it can be. doe-sn't sound like
B
dif-f'rent kind of ex-cel lence that's as strong as it can be. doe-sn't sound like

16
F+ Dm G F
S
ex-cel-lence, in-stead it sounds like you and me. It is an ex - cel lence, a dif-f'rent
A
ex-cel-lence, in-stead it sounds like you and me. ex - cel lence, a dif-f'rent
T
ex-cel-lence, in-stead it sounds like you and me. ex - cel lence, a dif-f'rent
B
ex-cel-lence, in-stead it sounds like you and me. ex - cel lence, a dif-f'rent

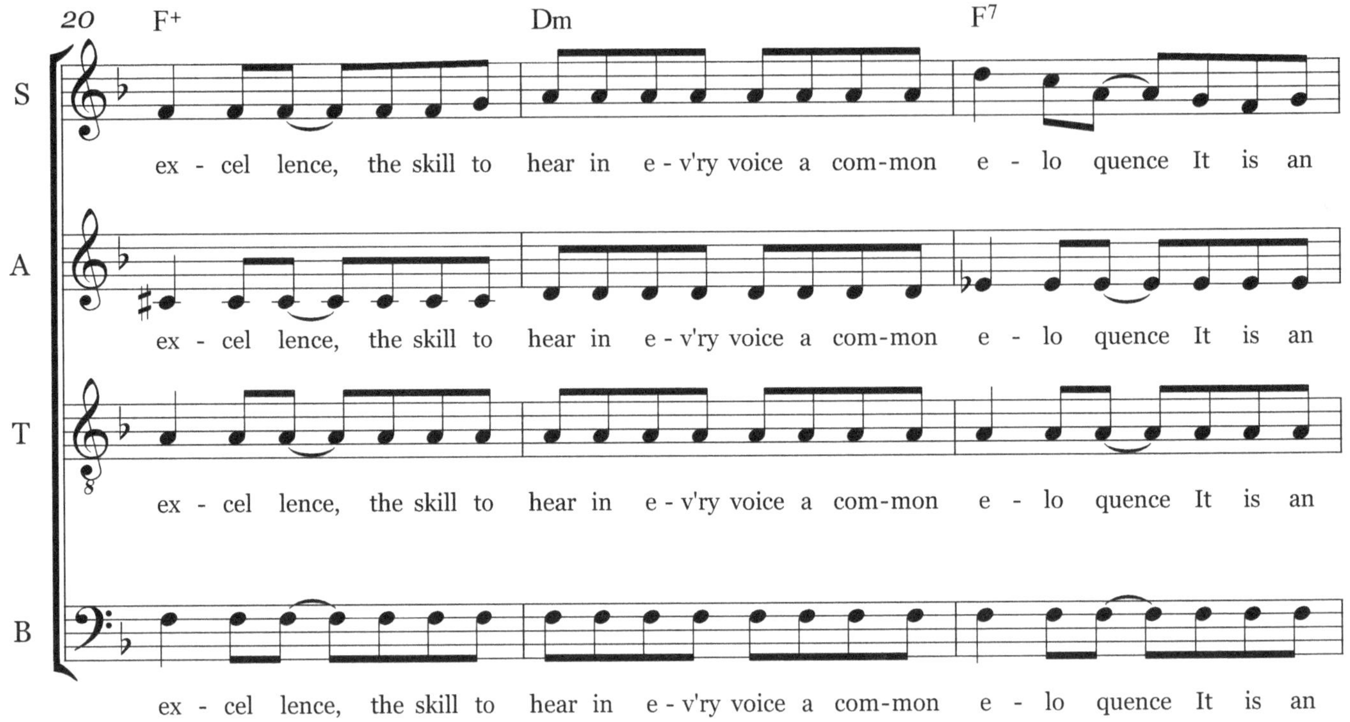
20
F+ Dm F7
S
A
T
B
ex - cel lence, the skill to hear in e - v'ry voice a com-mon e - lo quence It is an

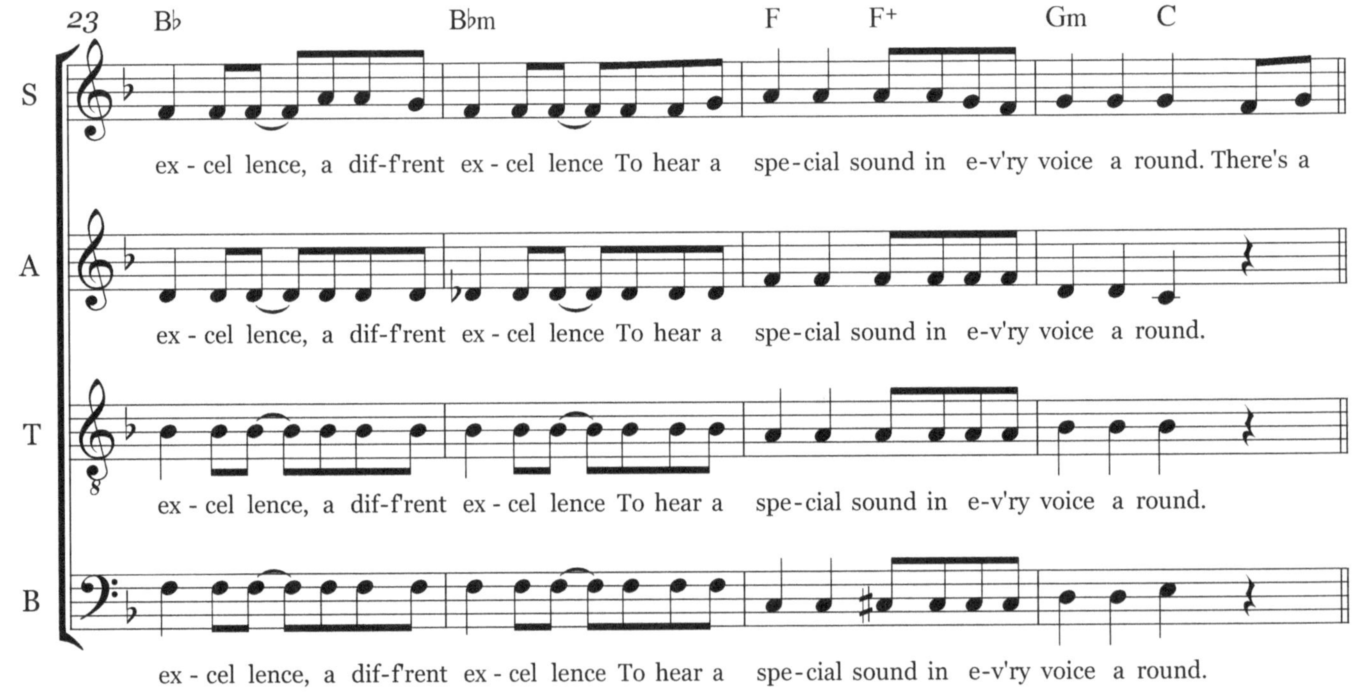
23
B♭ B♭m F F+ Gm C
S
A
T
B
ex - cel lence, a dif-f'rent ex - cel lence To hear a spe-cial sound in e-v'ry voice a round. There's a
ex - cel lence, a dif-f'rent ex - cel lence To hear a spe-cial sound in e-v'ry voice a round.

27
F F+ Dm F+ F
S
dif-f'rent kind of ex-cel lence that in-vites the world to sing. E-v'ry type of voice and
A
dif-f'rent kind of ex-cel lence that in-vites the world to sing. type of voice and
T
dif-f'rent kind of ex-cel lence that in-vites the world to sing. type of voice and
B
dif-f'rent kind of ex-cel lence that in-vites the world to sing. type of voice and
32
F+ Dm G F
S
song of choice is the ex - cel-lence they bring. There's a dif-f'rent kind of
A
song of choice is the ex - cel-lence they bring. dif-f'rent kind of
T
song of choice is the ex - cel-lence they bring. dif-f'rent kind of
B
song of choice is the ex - cel-lence they bring. dif-f'rent kind of

36
F+ Dm F+ F F+
S
ex-cel-lence where each sing - er has a worth. As we use our ears and learn to hear the im
A
ex-cel-lence where each sing - er has a worth. use our ears and learn to hear the im
T
ex-cel-lence where each sing - er has a worth. use our ears and learn to hear the im
B
ex-cel-lence where each sing - er has a worth. use our ears and learn to hear the im

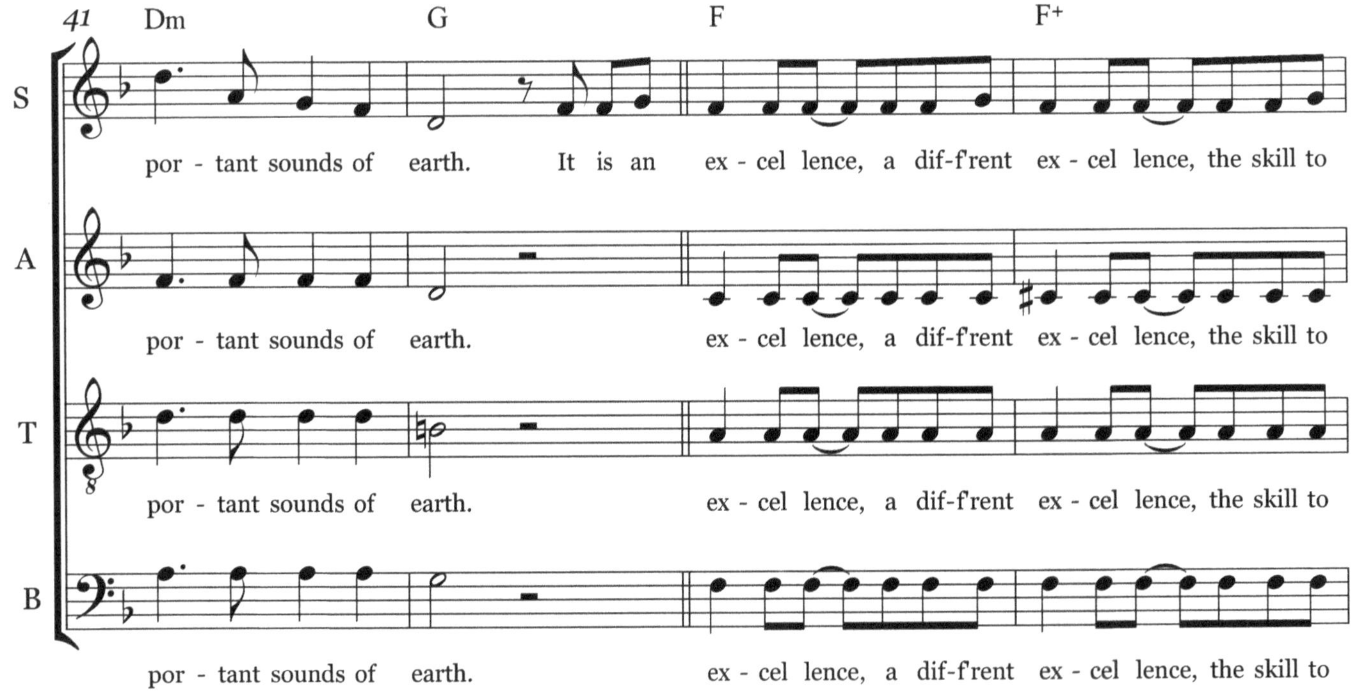
41
Dm G F F+
S
por - tant sounds of earth. It is an ex - cel lence, a dif-f'rent ex - cel lence, the skill to
A
por - tant sounds of earth. ex - cel lence, a dif-f'rent ex - cel lence, the skill to
T
por - tant sounds of earth. ex - cel lence, a dif-f'rent ex - cel lence, the skill to
B
por - tant sounds of earth. ex - cel lence, a dif-f'rent ex - cel lence, the skill to

45
Dm
F7
B♭
B♭m
S
A
T
B
hear in e-v'ry voice a com-mon e-lo quence It is an ex-cel lence, a dif-f'rent ex-cel lence To hear a
49
Monotone Moose
MM
Blah Blah Blah-Blah Blah Blah Blah Blah-Blah
F
F+
Gm
C
spe-cial sound in e-v'ry voice a-round.

54
MM
Blah
Sheep Translators
Sheep Choir
He says "Ex - cuse me Choir for E-v'ry- one, I don't mean to dis - rupt.

59
MM
Blah Blah Blah - Blah Blah
(choir delighted)
Sheep Choir
I'm a moose and I'm a mo-no-tone and I'd like to sign up.

Resolution

(from the "Excellence" choral dialectic)

Secretary Michael

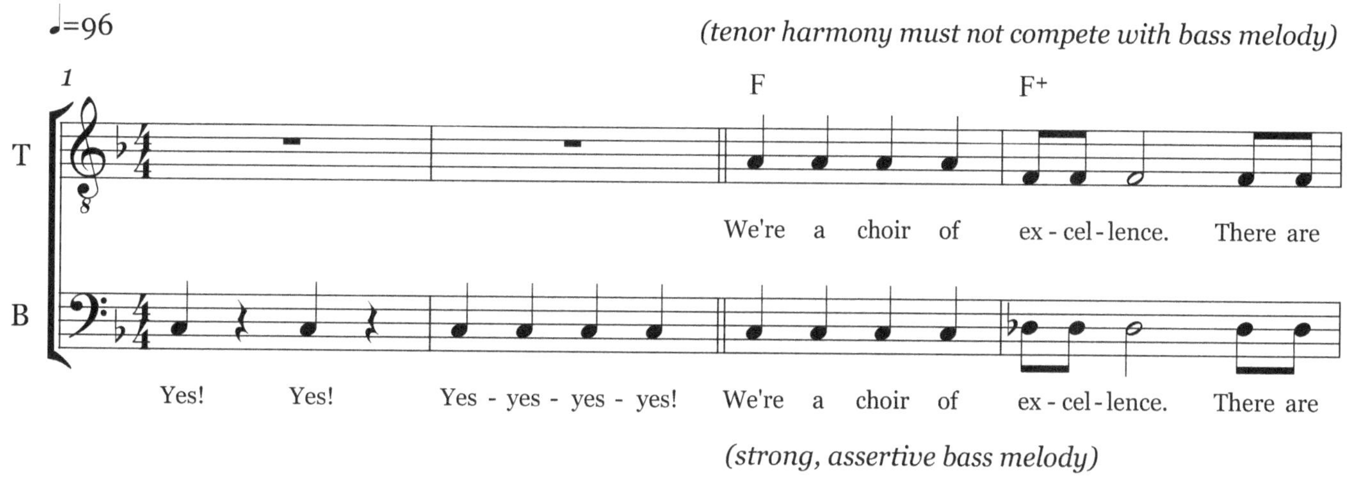

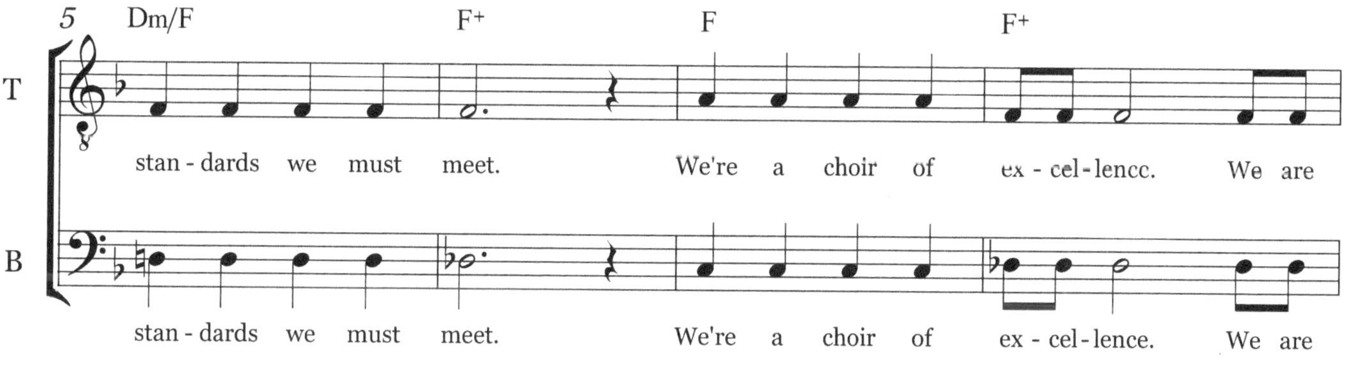

PD All works by Secretary Michael have been placed into the Public Domain. They may be freely copied and performed.

A
9
F
F+
S
We're a dif-f'rent kind of ex-cel-lence, you can
A
We're a dif-f'rent kind of ex-cel-lence, you can
Dm/F
F7
T
one of the e - lite. We're a choir of ex-cel-lence. You can
B
one of the e - lite. We're a choir of ex-cel-lence. You can
13
Dm
F+
F
F+
S
hear how we have grown. We're a dif-f'rent kind of ex-cel-lence with
A
hear how we have grown. We're a dif-f'rent kind of ex-cel-lence with
T
hear how we have grown. We're a choir of ex-cel-lence. with
B
hear how we have grown. We're a choir of ex-cel-lence. with

17
(all voices in unison)
F
F+
S
Moose the Mo - no - tone. We're a dif-f'rent kind of ex - cel - lence a -
A
Moose the Mo - no - tone. We're a dif-f'rent kind of ex - cel - lence a -
T
Moose the Mo - no - tone. We're a choir of ex - cel - lence. We're a -
B
Moose the Mo - no - tone. We're a choir of ex - cel - lence. We're a -

21
Dm
F+
F
F+
(all voices in unison)
S
bout to all break loose. We're a dif-f'rent kind of ex-cel-lence with Mo - no-tone the
A
bout to all break loose. We're a dif-f'rent kind of ex-cel-lence with Mo - no-tone the
T
bout to all break loose. We're a choir of ex-cel-lence with Mo - no-tone the
B
bout to all break loose. We're a choir of ex-cel-lence with Mo - no-tone the

B
Monotone Moose
(with impudent tone quality)
26
MM
S
A
T
B
Blah Blah Blah Blah Blah Blah Blah
Moose.
"No" (spoken)
"No" (spoken)
Moose.
Sheep (teaching)
Baa Baa (pure bleating)
Baa Baa (pure bleating)
Moose.
Moose.
32
MM
Sheep Choir
Blah Blah Blah Blah Blah-Blah Blah
Sheep Translators
Sheep (translating)
He says:"On - ly one crea-ture can bleat like a lamb.
39
MM
Sheep Choir
Blah Blah Blah-Blah Blah
Blah Blah Blah
O-thers should not have to pass that ex - am.

46
MM
Blah Blah
(Blah Blah Blah
Sheep Choir
On - ly one crea - ture can bleat like a lamb.
52
MM
Blah Blah Blah
Sheep Choir
I try and I try but that's not who I am.
T
TENORS
(strong, resolute) If
57
MM
T
peace and love there is to be, then we'll just have to change our key.

61
C♯7
Harmony Blossom
C
F♯
(melody must be clearly heard above animals)
Unis SATB
Unison (SATB)
It is an ex - cel - lence, a dif-f'rent
MM
MTONE MOOSE *
(exstatically)
Blah -blah - blah - blah Blah-blah-blah-blah
S1
C♯7
OWLS *
(OWLS: falsetto, not necessarily at written pitch; each "Hoo" ends with a Barred Owl-like drop in pitch)
We'll just have to change our key.
Hoo - hoo - hoo - hoo...
S2
BIRDS *
(whistled at pitch or ottava, with birdlike ornamentation)
We'll just have to change our key.
A1
CHKNS *
(nasal cackling, scooping into last two)
We'll just have to change our key.
Brawk-brawk-brawk-brawk BRAWK BRAWK
A2
SHEEP CHOIR *
(bleating tremolo)
We'll just have to change our key.
Baa
T1
DKEYS *
(DONKEYS: squeaky high pitchless "Hee" followed by a low, nasal, gravely honk)
We'll just have to change our key.
Hee
T2
DUCKS *
(nasal quacking)
We'll just have to change our key.
Quack, quack- quack.
B1
COWS *
(scoop into pitch from below)
We'll just have to change our key.
Moo
B2
PIGS *
(inhaled snorts)
We'll just have to change our key.
* *

** Most animals cannot be categorized as S, A, T, or B. Singers should choose their own animal.*

65
F♯+
D♯m
Unis SATB
ex - cel - lence,___ the skill to hear in e - v'ry voice a com-mon
MM
Blah - blah - blah - blah Blah-blah-blah-blah Blah - blah - blah - blah Blah-blah-blah-blah
Owls
Hoo - hoo - hoo - hoo...
Birds
(whistled...) (whistled...)
Chkns
Brawk brawk brawk-brawk BRAWK BRAWK Brawk brawk brawk-brawk BRAWK BRAWK
Sheep Choir
Baa Baa
Dkeys
Haw Hee-Haw Hee
Ducks
Quack, quack quack. Quack, quack quack.
Cows
Moo Moo
Pigs
* * * *

67
F#7
B
Unis SATB
e - lo - quence It is an ex - cel - lence, a dif-f'rent
MM
Blah - blah - blah - blah Blah-blah-blah-blah Blah - blah - blah - blah Blah-blah-blah-blah
Owls
Hoo - hoo - hoo - hoo...
Birds
(whistled...)
(whistled...)
Chkns
Brawk brawk brawk-brawk BRAWK BRAWK Brawk brawk brawk-brawk BRAWK BRAWK
Sheep Choir
Baa
Baa
Dkeys
Haw
Hee-Haw
Hee
Ducks
Quack, quack quack.
Quack, quack quack.
Cows
Moo
Moo
Pigs
* * * *

69
Bm
F♯
F♯+
Unis SATB
ex - cel - lence___ To hear a spe - cial sound in e - v'ry
MM
Blah - blah - blah - blah Blah blah blah blah Blah - blah - blah - blah Blah - blah - blah blah
Owls
Hoo - hoo - hoo hoo...
Birds
(whistled...)
(whistled...)
Chkns
Brawk brawk brawk brawk BRAWK BRAWK brawk brawk BRAWK brawk brawk BRAWK
Sheep Choir
Baa
Baa
Dkeys
Haw
Hee-Haw
Hee
Ducks
Quack, quack quack.
Quack, Quack Quack, Quack
Cows
Moo
Moo
Pigs
* * * *

71
G♯m
C♯7
D
F♯
Unis1 SATB div.
voice a - round It is an ex - cel - lence, a dif-f'rent
Unis2 SATB
Unison 2 (SATB)
(strong entrance)
We're a choir of
MM
(MM pants exhaustedly with tongue hanging out)
Blah - blah - blah - blah Blah blah blah blah
Owls
Hoo - hoo - hoo - hoo...
Birds
(whistled...)
(whistled...)
Chkns
Brawk brawk brawk brawk Brawk brawk brawk brawk Brawk brawk brawk brawk BRAWK BRAWK
Sheep Choir
Baa
Baa
Dkeys
Haw
Hee-Haw
Hee
Ducks
Quack, Quack Quack, Quack Quack, quack quack.
Cows
Moo
Moo
Pigs

73
F♯+
D♯m
Unis1 SATB div.
ex - cel - lence,___ the skill to hear in e - v'ry voice a com-mon
Unis2 SATB
ex - cel - lence. There are stan - dards we must
MM
Blah - blah - blah - blah Blah-blah-blah-blah Blah - blah - blah - blah Blah-blah-blah-blah
Owls
Hoo - hoo - hoo - hoo...
Birds
(whistled...)
(whistled...)
Chkns
Brawk brawk brawk-brawk BRAWK BRAWK Brawk brawk brawk-brawk BRAWK BRAWK
Sheep Choir
Baa
Baa
Dkeys
Haw
Hee-Haw
Hee
Ducks
Quack, quack quack.
Quack, quack quack.
Cows
Moo
Moo
Pigs
* * * *

75
F♯7(omit5)/E
B
Unis1 SATB div.
e - lo - quence It is an ex - cel - lence, a dif-f'rent
Unis2 SATB
meet. We're a choir of
MM
Blah - blah - blah - blah Blah-blah-blah-blah Blah - blah - blah - blah Blah-blah-blah-blah
Owls
Hoo - hoo - hoo - hoo...
Birds
(whistled...) (whistled...)
Chkns
Brawk brawk brawk-brawk BRAWK BRAWK Brawk brawk brawk-brawk BRAWK BRAWK
Sheep Choir
Baa Baa
Dkeys
Haw Hee-Haw Hee
Ducks
Quack, quack quack. Quack, quack quack.
Cows
Moo Moo
Pigs
* * * *

77
Bm
F♯
F♯+
Unis1 SATB
div.
ex - cel - lence___ on a ver - y dif - f'rent_
Unis2 SATB
ex - cel - lence on a ver - y dif - f'rent
MM
Blah - blah - blah - blah Blah blah-blah blah Blah - blah - blah blah Blah - blah - blah blah
Owls
Hoo - hoo - hoo hoo...
Birds
(whistled...) (whistled...)
Chkns
Brawk brawk brawk brawk BRAWK BRAWK brawk brawk BRAWK brawk brawk BRAWK
Sheep Choir
Baa Baa
Dkeys
Haw Hee-Haw Hee
Ducks
Quack, quack quack. Quack Quack Quack Quack
Cows
Moo Moo
Pigs

79
G♯m
C♯7
E
F♯
Unis1 SATB
div.
Unis2 SATB
MM
Owls
Birds
Chkns
Sheep Choir
Dkeys
Ducks
Cows
Pigs
street.
ANIMALS ONLY
street.
ANIMALS ONLY
(panting exhaustedly)
Blah
hoo - hoo - HOO...
(whistled...)
(whistled...)
Brawk-brawk-brawk-brawk Brawk
BRAWK BRAWK
Baa
Baa
Ba - ba - baa
ba
Haw
Quack Quack Quack Quack
Quack-quack Quack
Moo
Moo

ANIMALS ONLY

(ducks and sheep have melody)

ANIMALS ONLY

(ducks and sheep have melody)

87
C♯
F♯
D♯m
Unis SATB
Each breath we take, each sound we make, may
MM
Blah
Blah
Owls
hoo-hoo - HOO...
hoo-hoo - HOO...
hoo-hoo - HOO...
Birds
(whistled...)
(whistled...)
(whistled...)
Chkns
BRAWK BRAWK
BRAWK BRAWK
BRAWK BRAWK
Sheep Choir
Baa
Baa
Baa
Dkeys
Hee Haw
Ducks
Quack
Quack - quack
Quack - quack
Cows
Moo
Moo
Moo
Pigs
* *
* *
* *

90
B
F♯
Unis SATB
ex - cel - lent they be. For in the end the
MM
Blah Blah Blah
Owls
hoo - hoo - HOO... hoo - hoo - HOO...
Birds
(whistled...) (whistled...) (whistled...)
Chkns
BRAWK BRAWK BRAWK BRAWK BRAWK BRAWK
Sheep Choir
Baa Baa Baa
Dkeys
Hee-Haw
Ducks
Quack - quack Quack - quack Quack - quack
Cows
Moo Moo Moo
Pigs
* * * *

93
D♯m
G♯m
C♯7
F♯
Unis SATB
song we send is a piece of you and me.
Unis1 SATB
div.
Unis2 SATB
Each
MM
Blah
Blah
Owls
hoo-hoo - HOO...
hoo-hoo - HOO...
Birds
(whistled...)
(whistled...)
(whistled...)
Chkns
BRAWK BRAWK
BRAWK BRAWK
BRAWK BRAWK
Sheep Choir
Baa
Baa
Baa
Dkeys
Hee-Haw
Ducks
Quack - quack
Quack - quack
Quack - quack
Cows
Moo
Moo
Moo
Pigs

96
F
F♯
D♯m7
B
C♯7
Unis1 SATB
div.
We are the Choir for E - v'ry -
Unis2 SATB
breath we take, each sound we make, may ex - cel - lent they
MM
Blah - blah - blah Blah - blah - blah Blah - blah - blah
Owls
hoo - hoo - HOO... hoo - hoo - HOO... hoo - hoo - HOO...
Birds
(whistled...) (whistled...) (whistled...)
Chkns
BRAWK BRAWK BRAWK BRAWK BRAWK BRAWK
Sheep Choir
Baa Baa Baa
Dkeys
Ducks
Quack - quack Quack - quack Quack - quack
Cows
Moo Moo Moo
Pigs
* * * *

99
F♯
G♯m
A♯m
Unis1 SATB
div.
one. Work - ing to - ge - ther to
Unis2 SATB
be We're work - ing to - ge - ther to
MM
Blah - blah - blah
Owls
hoo-hoo - HOO... hoo-hoo - HOO... hoo-hoo - HOO...
Birds
(whistled...) (whistled...) (whistled...)
Chkns
BRAWK BRAWK BRAWK BRAWK BRAWK BRAWK
Sheep Choir
Baa Baa Baa
Dkeys
Hee-Haw
Ducks
Quack - quack Quack - quack Quack - quack
Cows
Moo Moo Moo
Pigs
* * * * * *

102
B
C♯(sus4)
C♯
F♯
Unis1 SATB
get the song sung. We all be -
div.
Unis2 SATB
get the song sung. We all be -
MM
Blah - blah - blah Blah - blah - blah
Owls
hoo-hoo-HOO... hoo-hoo-HOO... hoo-hoo-HOO...
Birds
(whistled...) (whistled...) (whistled...)
Chkns
BRAWK BRAWK BRAWK BRAWK BRAWK BRAWK
Sheep Choir
Baa Baa Baa
Dkeys
Hee-Haw
Ducks
Quack - quack Quack - quack Quack - quack
Cows
Moo Moo Moo
Pigs
* * * *

105
A♯m
D♯m
B
Unis1 SATB
div.
lieve, so - pra - no to bass,
Unis2 SATB
pra - no to bass,
MM
Blah - blah - blah Blah - blah - blah
Owls
hoo-hoo - HOO... hoo-hoo - HOO... hoo-hoo - HOO...
Birds
(whistled...) (whistled...) (whistled...)
Chkns
BRAWK BRAWK BRAWK BRAWK BRAWK BRAWK
Sheep Choir
Baa Baa Baa
Dkeys
Hee-Haw
Ducks
Quack - quack Quack - quack Quack - quack
Cows
Moo Moo Moo
Pigs
* * * *

108
F♯
D♯m
B
Unis1 SATB
that e - v'ry sing - er should be gi - ven a
div.
Unis2 SATB
that e - v'ry sing - er should be gi - ven a
MM
Blah - blah - blah Blah - blah - blah Blah - blah - blah
Owls
hoo - hoo - HOO... hoo - hoo - HOO... hoo - hoo - HOO...
Birds
(whistled...) (whistled...) (whistled...)
Chkns
BRAWK BRAWK BRAWK BRAWK BRAWK BRAWK
Sheep Choir
Baa Baa Baa
Dkeys
Ducks
Quack - quack Quack - quack Quack - quack
Cows
Moo Moo Moo
Pigs
* * * *

111
F♯
G
F♯
A♯m
Unis1 SATB
place.
Working together to
div.
Unis2 SATB
place.
Working together to
MM
Blah - blah - blah
Blah - blah - blah
Owls
hoo-hoo - HOO...
hoo-hoo - HOO...
hoo-hoo - HOO...
Birds
(whistled...)
(whistled...)
(whistled...)
Chkns
BRAWK BRAWK
BRAWK BRAWK
BRAWK BRAWK
Sheep Choir
Baa
Baa
Baa
Dkeys
Hee-Haw
Ducks
Quack - quack
Quack - quack
Quack - quack
Cows
Moo
Moo
Moo
Pigs

114
D♯m
B
F♯
Unis1 SATB
get the song sung, We are the
div.
Unis2 SATB
get the song sung, We are the
MM
Blah - blah - blah Blah Blah - blah - blah
Owls
hoo - hoo - HOO... Hoo... hoo - hoo - HOO...
Birds
(whistled...) (whistled...) (whistled...)
Chkns
BRAWK BRAWK BRAWK BRAWK BRAWK
Sheep Choir
Baa Baa Baa
Dkeys
Ducks
Quack - quack Quack Quack - quack
Cows
Moo Moo Moo
Pigs
* *

117
D♯m
G♯m7
Unis1 SATB
Choir for E - - - -
div.
Unis2 SATB
Choir for E - - - -
MM
Blah - blah - blah
Owls
hoo - hoo - HOO...
hoo - hoo - hoo - hoo - hoo - hoo
Birds
(whistled...)
(whistled...)
Chkns
BRAWK BRAWK
Brawk - brawk - brawk - brawk Brawk - brawk -
Sheep Choir
Baa Baa Baa Baa
Dkeys
Hee - Haw
Ducks
Quack - quack Quack Quack Quack
Cows
Moo Moo
Pigs
* * * *

119
C♯7
F♯
Unis1 SATB
div.
- - - v'ry - one!
Unis2 SATB
- - - v'ry - one!
MM
Blah -blah Blah - blah Blah - blah
Owls
hoo - hoo - hoo - hoo - hoo - hoo hoo - hoo - hoo - hoo - hoo - hoo
Birds
(whistled...) (whistled...)
Chkns
Brawk-brawk - brawk-brawk Brawk-brawk - Brawk-brawk - brawk-brawk Brawk-brawk -
Sheep Choir
Baa Baa Baa Baa
Dkeys
Hee-Haw Hee-Haw Hee-Haw Hee -
Ducks
Quack Quack Quack Quack Quack Quack
Cows
Moo Moo
Pigs
* * * *

121
Unis1 SATB
div.
Unis2 SATB
MM
Blah -blah Blah - blah Blah - blah Blah -blah Blah - blah Blah - blah Blah!
Owls
hoo - hoo - hoo - hoo - hoo - hoo hoo - hoo - hoo - hoo - hoo - hoo Hoo!
Birds
(whistled...)
(whistled...)
Chkns
Brawk-brawk - brawk-brawk Brawk-brawk - Brawk-brawk - brawk-brawk Brawk-brawk BRAWK!
Sheep Choir
Dkeys
Haw Hee-Haw Hee-Haw Hee - Haw Hee-Haw Hee-Haw Haw!
Ducks
Quack Quack Quack Quack Quack Quack Quack!
Cows
Moo Moo Moo
Pigs
* * * * * * * *

Notes on the "Excellence" choral dialectic

Thanks for taking a chance on this piece. It's a rare person who would choose to work on a choral piece with the phrase "Animal Choir" in its title.

Although the various animals appear to be written in specific voices (such as soprano, alto, tenor or bass), in reality most animals are all over the map. For example, the "Pigs" have been put down with the basses. However a soprano can surely snort (inhaling, using mouth shape to create pitch) as well as a bass. The "Birds" have been put up with the sopranos. However a bass can surely whistle as well as a soprano. Some animals (especially the "Sheep" and the "Cows") do belong where they were assigned (alto and bass, respectively). However others (especially the "Owls", "Birds", and "Pigs") could have been put anywhere. It was just the logistics of scoring that they ended-up where they did. The point of this is that the singers should pick whatever animal best suits them, regardless of the staff it appears on.

I chose 8 animals for our Animal Choir so that each SATB voice would have two animals. I now realize that this makes no sense. In my next life I'll pick fewer animals.

<u>OWLS</u>: There's a Barred Owl that I often hear near my home. It's a fascinating sound. I'm not sure that I have an adequate vocabulary to describe it. It's a "thrown" sound - a projected falsetto. Years ago I wrote another song for Animal Choir ("We are the Animals of the Planet Earth") for the musical "Twimfina". There were no owls in that song because owls are not vegetarians - they would eat the birds and the chickens. This time I wasn't such a purist.

<u>BIRDS</u>: 100% whistled; it might be nice to ad lib some birdlike coloratura; some birds can be quite acrobatic with their sounds;

<u>CHICKENS</u>: a nasal "Brawk", occasionally with an upward-scooping pitch;

<u>SHEEP</u>: a tremolo is probably the main feature of a bleat; the sheep have been assigned an alto voice; it's probably best to have several sheep in the section because they divide into 2-part harmony;

<u>DONKEYS</u>: don't worry about a pitch on the short, squeaky-high "Hee" part; the low, gravelly, foghorn-like "Haw" doesn't absolutely need a pitch, but it would be nice if one could be found down there in the basement;

<u>DUCKS</u>: nasal and piercing;

<u>COWS</u>: low bass tones, approached by a scoop;

<u>PIGS</u>: inhaled snorts; pitch can be created by mouth shape; probably serves more as a percussion instrument; as with all the animal voices, there's something humorous about it;

Recent Works by Secretary Michael

Jo Puma - Wild Choir Music
Collection of 36 traditional "Sacred Harp" arrangements with new secular lyrics for our diverse society. This collection has removed the 3 barriers that have kept this music out of our schools: inappropriate lyrics, poor shape-note legibility, and nonstandard use of standard solfege names. Now we all have a chance to experience this exciting early American music. (Book available; check for free download: www.machinistsunion.org/works.html)

Secular Hymnal
Collection of 144 favorite hymn tunes from around the world. The hymn tunes have been re-notated and given thoughtful egalitarian lyrics that promote peace. Many public schools use them for choral sight-reading practice. Available in both unison/guitar and SATB choir editions. Now we all have a chance to share in these musical treasures. (Books available; check for free download: www.machinistsunion.org/works.html)

Twimfina
A peace-themed musical play for singing groups of all ages. The story is about a young woman named "Twimfina" (an acronym for "The World Is My Family, I'm Not Afraid") who runs off to a hostile country. It is scored for voice and piano. The play is divided into 21 segments, many of which can stand alone. This allows an acting group to perform individual segments instead of the entire 2.5 hour play. (Book available; check for free download: www.machinistsunion.org/works.html)

Choral Dialectics
A "choral dialectic" is a 4-movement choral work (with or without instruments) in which a rational argument is battled-out musically. There's only one rule: every choral dialectic must use the following four titles for its four movements: "Principle" - "Argument" - "Counterargument" - "Resolution"
Secretary Michael has begun working on a series of 6 choral dialectics, some of which are available now; the rest will become available as they are completed in future years. (Books available; check for free downloads: www.machinistsunion.org/works.html)

Aren't We the Lucky Ones
A book-length story about a group of college science students who share an understanding that people don't truly have a free will. There are no "good people" or "bad people", just lucky and unlucky ones. This insight carries with it the responsibility to protect the "unlucky" from the wrath of the "lucky" . The students form a community in order to live out their ideals. (Book available - both paperback and digital).

Joy of Piggyback Songs
Dozens of fun, short choral works in which more than one melody is sung at the same time. Book (and free internet download) will become available after it is completed.

"Please help create public choirs that are free from religious and nationalistic content so that all singers feel welcome."

- Secretary Michael

www.ingramcontent.com/pod-product-compliance
Lightning Source LLC
Chambersburg PA
CBHW080530030426
42337CB00023B/4688
9781888712407